THE R
TO DRAW CARICATURES

THE RIGHT WAY TO DRAW CARICATURES

Mark Linley

RIGHT WAY

Typeset in 11/12pt Times by Letterpart Limited, Reigate, Surrey.
Printed and bound in Great Britain by Cox & Wyman Ltd., Reading, Berkshire.

The *Right Way* series is published by Elliot Right Way Books, Brighton Road, Lower Kingswood, Tadworth, Surrey, KT20 6TD, U.K. For information about our company and the other books we publish, visit our web site at www.right-way.co.uk

Dedication

To Pat, and everyone with a sense of humour.

Acknowledgements

Following pictures by John Ball:
77, 81, 83, 90, 92, 94, 116 and 117.

All the other pictures are by the author.

CONTENTS

CHAPTER   PAGE

1. HOW TO DRAW CARICATURES   9
What is a caricature? Drawing from life.
The famous. Be a wild child. Be positive.

2. WAYS AND MEANS   12
Look, look, look. What you will need. Pencil power.
A light or viewing box. The Queen and I. Assignments.

3. HOW TO HELP YOURSELF   16
Practice. Bag a good hooter. Assignments.

4. SLIGHTLY DONE, NOT BURNT   20
The Big Three. Big ears, floppy lugs. Big trap!
Eyes, brows and nose. Assignments.

5. FUN WITH FACES   27
Hairy. Stretch, flatten, push or pull. Start at the top.
Assignments.

6. GET OUT!   34
Work away. Collect faces. Assignments.

7. BIG HEAD, SMALL BODY   39
Put a bit of stick about. Known victims.
Add on. Assignments.

8. RETURN TO SCHOOL 46
Go to school. Be fast. Assignments.

9. FAMOUS FACES 53
Entertainers. 007. In the news. Assignments.

10. LATE GREATS 64
Enduring fame. A lovely double act. The first great comic.
A legendary lady. Home-grown late greats.
The King. Assignments.

11. TURN ON THE TELLY 75
How to draw from television. Television presenters.
A bit of spice. Class. New stars. Assignments.

12. PLEASE BE A SPORT 103
Fore! A sensational golfer. A world champion.
Everyone for tennis. The top man. We each have a hero.
Easy ones for you. Assignments.

13. MAKE A BIT OF DOSH 125
How to make money with caricatures. How to start.
Last hints.

1

HOW TO DRAW CARICATURES

The top caricaturists are those whose work you see in national newspapers, magazines and on television. The ability to caricature world famous celebrities, often with just a few telling lines, is a demanding skill. This art form can be learned in easy stages. You will find help-line sketches for many drawings in this book so take heart.

There are thousands of amateur caricaturists who gain satisfaction (and sometimes money) from drawing caricatures of people they know, meet or see around sometimes, maybe, in football, cricket, or other sports clubs.

In the past cigarette cards were widely used to promote the product via life-like caricatures of famous sportsmen. These have now become collectors' items.

Today the majority of published caricatures are life-like rather than like those produced at the pinnacle of this art.

I was once a member of the happy amateur brigade. My cartoons and caricatures of fellow ramblers led directly to my being asked to write and illustrate a first book. A similar happy experience could come your way.

I have designed this book to show inexperienced or beginner artists how to become competent caricaturists.

What is a caricature?
A caricature is defined, in my battered dictionary, as a grotesque comically exaggerated representation of a person. Also

as a ridiculously poor imitation or version of a person. I call them victims!

A poor imitation, of course, gives you a lot of freedom. Some of the best caricatures appear to have been drawn by backward children. Several students I once taught could naturally draw people in this sort of style. Quite often pupils amazed themselves by having a kind of built-in skill to make comical sketches of fellow humans.

Drawing from life

When some faces can be rapidly jotted down as grotesque or comical records, it's great fun for the artist. Victims, however, may not be overjoyed. Care is needed when you caricature anyone who is within thumping distance of yourself!

It is easier to produce a caricature from someone you know than to draw a famous person from a one-dimensional photograph. You can walk round your live victim, go in for a close look, chat and have a laugh.

The famous

Famous people are fair game for all caricaturists. Top caricaturists enjoy freedom to express what they, their editor, or boss think of anyone. To begin with, forget about making pictures which carry a message. This will naturally come as you progress.

Way back in British history some kings bribed caricaturists not to draw them. The artists concerned enjoyed great prestige and power.

We have all seen the high and mighty brought to earth by a brilliant cartoon. It can be said that political caricaturists do a darned good job. They all too often depict what most of us think. They highlight scandals, expose sleazy Members of Parliament. Fat Cats of industry have their inflated salaries mocked. Big-headed celebrities are not immune to a little wicked humour.

Be a wild child

If you have a wicked sense of humour and can draw like a child you might well have it made as a future brilliant caricaturist! But before you hit the big time there are a few tricks of the trade to learn. I will take you through simple stages of drawing before unleashing you on the world famous.

Be positive

If you, like tens of thousands of other readers, have read some of my other *Right Way To Draw* books, skip this paragraph about thinking positively. If not, you are about to learn the most important lesson ever. You can learn to do anything anyone else can do. How? Just by thinking that you can and never, never say or think that you can't. Especially when you really mean "I don't know how to". It's my job, which I love, to teach you how.

You have a most powerful computer inside your brain. It's called a subconscious mind, but all you need to know is that you programme it by the way you think. Send it the message "I can". Then it will become so. Here endeth the first vital lesson!

2

WAYS AND MEANS

In this chapter we will consider ways and means of drawing caricatures. It would be best for you to decide on one system then to stick to that until you have achieved your aim. Right?

Look, look, look
One of the most important qualities required for caricaturing is sound observation. Good observation is essential to all forms of art. You cannot draw anything if you are unable to see what shape or form your object is. If, for example, you want to draw a caricature of someone who is blessed with big ears, a crooked mouth, receding hairline and a broken nose then you have an easy-to-draw victim. On the other hand, a person with no outstanding features is difficult to caricature. The key to success is always in careful observation. That's common sense isn't it?

It's sometimes possible to depict a person's face by exaggerating just one or two features. Try to keep your drawing as simple as you can – and as funny as possible.

What you will need
You will not require much in the way of equipment in order to start your new skill. A 2B drawing pencil, medium eraser, a size A4 sketchpad or a packet of A4 typing paper (which is much cheaper to buy), a black fibre tip drawing pen, size .5, or similar instrument. A calligraphy pen is useful if you want to

have varied thicknesses of line in your masterpieces. For filling in large areas, called blocking in, you will require a small watercolour paint brush, size 5 or 6 and a small bottle of drawing ink. A size A5 pad would be useful to carry around to jot down your impression of different victims you may come across.

Pencil power

No two artists work in the same way. You will soon find what is best for you, but for those who have yet to get into a method, I will explain how *I* go about the job.

I always start with a good old drawing pencil, grade 2B, by scribbling a rough sketch on scrap paper. The object is to obtain a reasonable likeness of a victim's mouth, nose, eyes and eyebrows. When that has been achieved I place the rough drawing under a sheet of tracing paper then, still with a pencil, try to improve upon what has been done. This process is repeated with a face shape and body if required. I sometimes manage to get it right straight off but it usually needs several drawings in order to almost please me.

When the finished pencil caricature, on tracing paper, is arrived at, it is then transferred to drawing paper. This can be

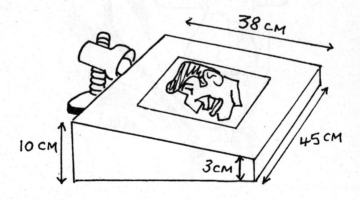

Fig. 1. A light or viewing box.

done by rubbing lead pencil on the reverse side of the sketch then using it like carbon paper to make an image onto typing or cartridge paper. The sketch is then ready to be inked in. Pencil marks are erased to leave a finished masterpiece.

A light or viewing box
The best way to transfer pencil work is, however, by using a light box. This is a gadget which can be made or bought. It's simply a box with a sloping top of semi-opaque material such as frosted glass. A small light in the box illuminates the original sketch from underneath. Inking in is then very easy.

My box is made of plastic. It was obtained by post from an

Fig. 2. Monarch.

art supplies company. Figure 1 will show you what it looks like.

The Queen and I

Take a quick look at figure 2. Do you think that my version of Britain's popular Queen could result in Mark Linley heading the Honours List? Perhaps not. But maybe Her Majesty will slip a tenner or two my way. Am I being too optimistic? Oh, well . . .

Notice in my sketch how certain facial features have been stretched in order to make a humorous portrait. We shall be returning to this sketch a little later in the book. Then you will see how a finished caricature is arrived at in easy stages.

Assignments

1. Try tracing any drawing then transferring it to cartridge paper.
2. Use the same method to copy the Queen caricature.

3

HOW TO HELP YOURSELF

How can you help yourself to become a good caricaturist? By working through each assignment in this book. The temptation is to skip these but those readers who have a business-like approach have been the ones who have made the quickest progress.

Study as many newspaper and magazine caricatures as you can get hold of. Include funny cartoon characters because caricaturing is simply the next stage. Copy those which you like then re-draw them in your own style or way. By this I mean put a bit of yourself into what you create. Remember that most beginners are much too hard on themselves so expect a few hiccups to start with but never despair. Enjoy what you do, that is the big secret of most success. You can get there. As your graphic skill improves you can begin to think of relevant details to add to your caricature that will enhance the humour. Look for the story behind *every* face.

Practice
My friend and I, when out and about, look for people who strike us as being good cartoon victims. "That's a good one," we say to each other reaching for our pencils. You can mentally practise each time you set eyes on a fellow human. When you read your newspaper or magazine, pause to think how you could make a comical drawing of people seen in print.

I noticed (during my teaching days) that some beginner artists were rather shy about making grotesque drawings of the famous but had no such feeling about doing a jokey sketch of their best and most understanding pal. Others were just the opposite. They avoided sketching those they knew but joyfully had a go at famous personalities. It appeared to take different people different ways. I hope that you will tackle anybody in as comical a way as possible.

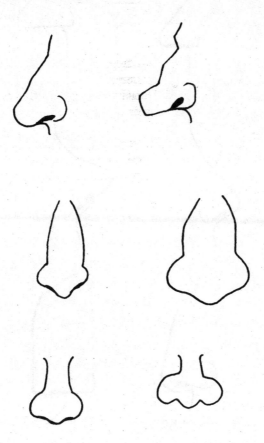

Fig. 3. Exaggerated Noses.

Bag a good hooter

Some caricaturists begin by first drawing the nose of their victim. This is quite a good starting point and not too hard. I

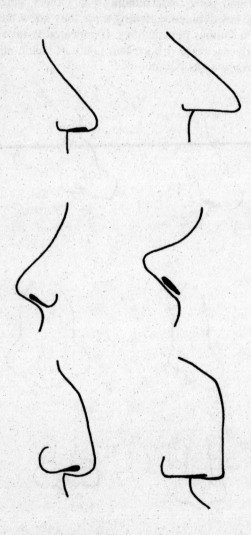

Fig. 4. Try stretching noses further!

would like you now to make your first venture into your new art form by studying my sketches in figure 3. The life-like nose is on the left hand side of the page with my caricature of it on the right. Draw your version of the exaggerated noses.

Next go to figure 4 and repeat the exercise. Twenty minutes is the time adults hold their concentration most effectively. Keep to this and you will produce your best work for longer spells. Take a tea or coffee break. You have earned it.

Assignments
1. From a photograph draw a caricature of a nose.
2. Exaggerate the nose of someone you know.
3. Make a caricature of your own nose from the front and side (profile).

4

SLIGHTLY DONE, NOT BURNT!

Now that you have had a little drawing practice on noses you are ready to move on to sketching other facial features. In this chapter you will extend what you did in the last session.

To begin with concentrate on just slightly exaggerating faces. Think of it as being a bit like cooking. Slightly boil but do not burn to a cinder!

The Big Three

From my own experience I have learnt that in order to obtain a likeness in a face, whether drawn as a straight portrait, cartoon or caricature, it is important to depict the nose, mouth and eyes, including brows, more or less correctly. If this isn't done the drawing will fail.

To show you the importance of accurately drawing the Big Three I have caricatured the face of world famous Hollywood film star Sylvester Stallone. He is the actor who created the fictional character Rambo. The first movie was so successful that follow-ups of the same character were made. Rambo seems to have set a fashion for current film heroes. Many of them now appear to wear tatty vests, grubby headbands and have over-developed arm muscles!

Examine figure 5. See how I have used the heavily hooded eyes, hooked nose, distinctive lips, strong eyebrows, headband, ears and hair style to caricature this wonderful face. Try to copy this illustration for a little advanced practice or wait until I show

Fig. 5. Rambo's face.

you how to add a body on to this face, later on page 44.

Big ears, floppy lugs
You will see, in figure 6, normal ears on the left hand side then slightly exaggerated drawing of these ears on the right of the page. See if you can stretch the examples just a bit further but remember that your caricature ought to resemble the originals.

Some famous people naturally have larger than average ears. Prince Charles is, perhaps, one of the best known examples. This is due to caricaturists depicting the poor man as owning quite enormous lugs. In actual fact the Prince's ears are not all that large. Having stated that, I have gone along with the crowd by caricaturing Charles in the accepted way. See figure 7. Have a shot at drawing the Prince.

Big trap!
Our faces, as with all our body bits and pieces, vary from those of other humans. It's just as well or we would all be identical clones.

When mouths are drawn from life it is usual for the artist not to draw in each individual tooth. See figure 8. The exception to this rule is when teeth are a definite feature to pick on. Lips are exaggerated in shape and quite often in size. Big mouths are

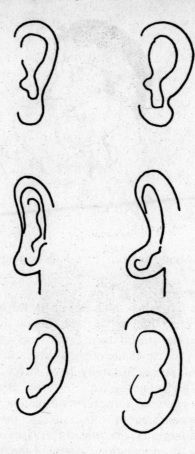

Fig. 6. Try your hand at ears!

common to caricatures. This is shown in my sketches.

A few famous people were born with larger than normal mouths. Pop star, Mick Jagger is one well-known example. Mouths are a feature to make use of in many caricatures. A mouth can be distinctive when seen from the front or side. Have another look at Rambo, figure 5.

A mouth may be unusual in shape or size. If viewed in

Fig. 7. Prince Charles's famous ears.

profile, it may reveal that the upper lip is much larger than the lower lip. Study the second drawing down in figure 8. A lower lip could be larger than the upper one, or both lips might stick out a lot. Also revealed will be protruding upper, lower or both sets of teeth. These conditions will always cause a lip or lips to pop forward.

Teeth can be straight, crooked, missing, chipped or gapped. Gums may be hidden when a person smiles, or fully revealed. All these small points should be observed, remembered and roughly sketched in order to produce a well-drawn caricature.

Draw your version of examples in figure 8. Notice how lips can be shaded by using fine lines.

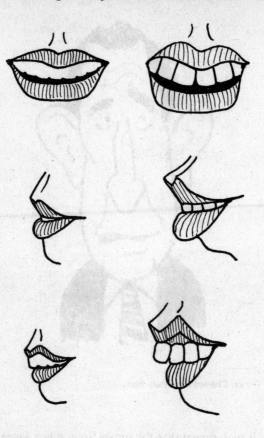

Fig. 8. Mouths made bigger.

Eyes, brows and nose

To extend what you have now done study the half faces, profile, in figure 9. Once more I have taken normal faces, on the left of the illustration, and exaggerated them a little to produce the drawings shown on the right of the page.

Look carefully at them to decide for yourself how much or how little each feature has been used to make a caricature. Ask yourself if noses, for instance, have been shortened, lengthened

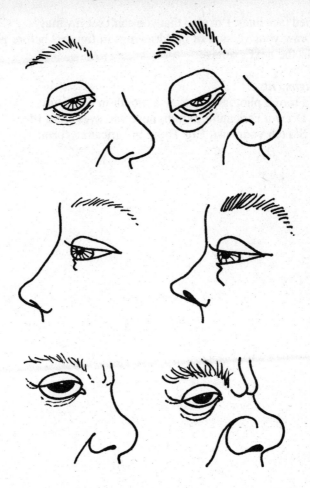

Fig. 9. Nose, eye and brows, slightly stretched.

or made bulbous. What about eyes? Are they drawn larger, smaller or the same. Eyebrows can be a distinctive feature in some people. Think of Charlie Chaplin for example. When brows are very noticeable they are very helpful to the caricaturist. The same is true of eyelids, bags under eyes, and deeply etched face lines. I'm glad that you can't see my mug!

Draw your version of my drawings in figure 9 before going on to the next exercise.

Assignments
1. From a photograph draw a mouth in caricature.
2. Draw a caricature mouth, nose and eyes from life.
3. Sketch your own Big Three in caricature form.

5

FUN WITH FACES

In this chapter you take another small step towards your goal by learning how to caricature whole heads.

Hairy

There are many ways of caricaturing hair. One artist may do the job making hair rather solid looking, another might sketch in just a few wispy strands whilst others seem to scribble in weird shapes and patterns. You should try to evolve what suits you. Study how different caricaturists work.

Have a look at figure 10. Notice, top left, how broken lines have been used to draw a woman's hair. Opposite is a man's thatch, drawn then blocked in. Second one down, left, is another female style but drawn as a series of leaf-like shapes. On the right of this illustration is a Spice Girl type style. This was sketched by using small wavy lines. Third drawing down, left, is a curly haired lady. It was done with controlled scribble made up of little circles. On the right a bearded gentleman. This type of hair is simply drawn as outlines. Bottom left shows a girl's style of short cut produced by solid lines as is the hair on the right. Draw these hair styles as quickly as you can. Why? Because quite often the lightning sketch will produce the best way of caricaturing.

To get an idea of how a hair style suits a particular face I have drawn six examples for figure 11. Can you spot two famous dials? That's right. Baroness Thatcher and that superb

Fig. 10. Different ways to depict hair.

actor, Sir John Gielgud. Notice how I have exaggerated face shapes in order to make caricatures of the heads. Now test your talent by sketching out your versions of figure11.

Beards and moustaches are treated the same way as head hair. Some people are living caricatures. I regard actor Buster Merryfield as one of this delightful bunch. He's one of the famous TV cast who created *Only Fools and Horses*. I have

Fig. 11. Add a face to a hairstyle.

drawn a caricature of Buster by simply exaggerating the magnificent beard he has, then popping legs and hands sticking out from it. See figure 12. Copy this for fun.

Stretch, flatten, push, or pull
What can a would-be caricaturist do with a face shape? Quite a lot. A round face, for example, can be made to look like a perfect circle. A long, thin face could be sketched as a long

Fig. 12. Buster Merryfield.

strip. Some features can be pulled out: chins, cheeks, fore-
heads, necks and throats. The same features could also, if
required, be pulled in. Once more it's all about looking
properly before dashing away with your pencil. Figure 13
illustrates various face shapes which have been stretched a
little. Try your hand at these.

One of the best caricaturists, to me, is Gary Smith. His
brilliant drawings appear regularly in national newspapers
and magazines. He has an enviable talent for using simple
shapes to capture the character of whoever he draws. Try to

Fig. 13. How to stretch faces.

collect then study his work. But remember that there is only one Gary.

Start at the top
To try out my method of working I would like you to draw a caricature of the Queen. This is figure 2 in the first chapter, but is reproduced here to show the different stages of drawing

Fig. 14.   Above: First rough drawing.
          Below: Face roughed in.

which went into it. Study figures 14 and 15. Now use your
own style and skill to depict Her Majesty.

   If you have already produced the Queen as a caricature turn
your attention to Sylvester Stallone and Baroness Thatcher.

Assignments
1. From a photograph draw a whole face as a caricature.
2. Repeat the same exercise on a famous face from the last
    two chapters.
3. From life draw a whole face caricature.

Fig. 15. Finished caricature.

6

GET OUT!

Without doubt, drawing from life is the quickest way to become a competent artist. The more you can do this the better you will be. Try to discipline yourself to carry a small sketch pad and pencil with you. Then get out to draw the many victims you will come across. Your progress could amaze you!

Work away

I have drawn over twenty people from life in half an hour. The majority of this time was spent just observing my victims. The drawing time per caricature was roughly 30 seconds. You could equal my score easily with a little practice, but, to begin with, allow yourself 5 minutes per person.

When you see a possible victim ask yourself which facial features you first notice, what build is the person, what clothes are worn and which characteristics could be used? With practice all this information is taken on board in a few seconds. Then, without further observation, you quickly jot down a first impression.

There are many places which you could visit to further your skill. Shopping centres and malls are super spots to hide away in to observe the human race. Markets and sports meetings also provide good vantage points for caricaturists. Just think about where you go.

Collect faces

Your outdoor experiences should begin with a small collection of faces caricatured. It's good fun drawing these. I have

Fig. 16. A page of faces.

popped out myself to produce the faces shown in figure 16. Notice how hair has been drawn. My attention was first drawn, in fact, to the distinctive hair styles. I made these a feature to

Fig. 17. Start with rough sketches.

exaggerate. The male victim had a distinctive nose, bless him!

The first rough drawing you make is usually the most important because your finished sketch depends on its accuracy. Sometimes the first impression is the one to use as a caricature. Figure 17 shows how my roughs looked before turning into those in figure 16. Study these drawings before you draw your versions. Try to improve on my sketches.

Figure 18 is the result of catching a very good-to-draw group of victims. They were all so different from each other. Nose, eyes, brows and hats were exaggerated to create the top two

Fig. 18. Lovely victims!

gentlemen. Face shape, hair style and mouth attracted my attention when drawing the two ladies. See my rough sketches in figure 19 before you turn your talent onto these wonderful faces.

Fig. 19.   The important first impressions.

Assignments
1.   Draw a caricature of a lady shopper.
2.   Next draw a man shopping.
3.   Try to caricature a child.

7

BIG HEAD, SMALL BODY

Up to now you have concentrated your efforts on caricaturing faces. Now I want you to add on a body. In my (not too) humble opinion the difference between a cartoon and a caricature is in how the body is depicted. In almost every caricature the head is drawn much larger than the body. In a cartoon the proportions, which may be slightly exaggerated, are more or less to scale. Caricaturists tend to draw little bodies beneath the all important head. The bodies drawn are mostly accurate though miniaturised.

Put a bit of stick about
If you have had little experience of body drawing I suggest that you start by putting a bit of stick about. In other words begin by sketching stick figures which you then thicken out into a proper body shape.

In figure 20 you will see two stick figures. The dotted lines show how the sticks were thickened. This is a very useful trick in obtaining the correct body shape. The people in figure 21, drawn from life, reveal the finished illustration. Copy my stick figures to arrive at the same result.

Look at figure 22 for two more stick figures to work on. The whole bodies are shown in figure 23. These victims were drawn from life. Notice how hair and clothes have been drawn.

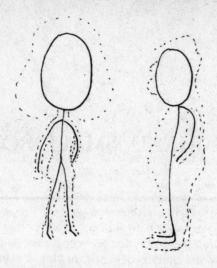

Fig. 20. Stick figures will help you.

Fig. 21. Sticks made whole.

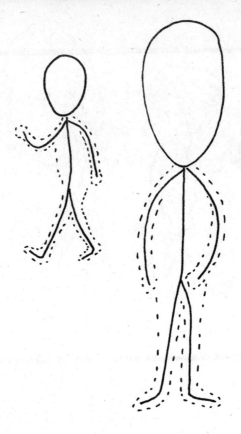

Fig. 22. More stick figures.

Known victims

As mentioned previously, to begin with it is easier to caricature someone you know. An advantage of using friends as
models is that you can ask them to pose for you briefly. This
may involve you in much funny but useless banter. It's part of
life isn't it? Be prepared for your mate suddenly to become
self-conscious or "camera shy". Use your humour to relax
your victim. "If you don't stop fidgeting about I'll thump

Fig. 23. The finished drawings.

you," is a line bound to get results!

My victims for figure 24 are chums met on a golf course. One of them, when not playing golf, fishes, or watches football, cricket or boxing on television. I wonder how he manages to arrive on the golf course bright-eyed and fresh

Fig. 24. Caricature those you know.

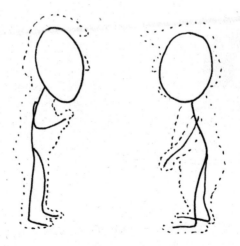

Fig. 25. Stick figure help lines.

enough to beat me. I enjoyed myself exaggerating the figures of my chums. I shall beg for mercy when they see my drawings!

Seriously though, my best sketches of friends have been made when they were not aware of what I was up to. After studying the help lines in figure 25 I should like you to draw a ridiculously poor imitation of the two sporting gents.

Add on

Fig. 26.   Give Rambo a body!

Fig. 27.   A stick Rambo could help you.

It's time for you to give Rambo a bit of a body as I have done in figure 26. I have lightly drawn in the face in figure 27 to help with your sketch. Give Prince Charles the full treatment as in figures 28 and 29. Finish this section with a caricature of him before taking a break.

Fig. 28. The full Charlie.

Fig. 29. A sticky start for Charlie.

Assignments
1. From life draw two caricatures that include the body.
2. After watching children draw caricatures of two of them.
3. Try sketching a rapid caricature of a famous person.

8

RETURN TO SCHOOL

When caricaturing children you can be quite savage in the way you portray them. Remember how the late great Ronald Searle drew the St Trinians girls? Or how Giles caricatured small babies? A week ago I happened to see a baby who resembled a Giles drawing. Poor little soul. I have to confess, however, to laughing my head off when I drew my version of it. What a sometimes wicked sense of humour I have. See figure 30.

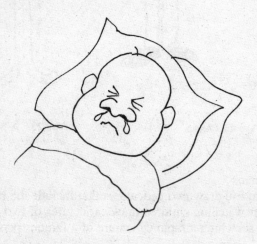

Fig. 30.   Poor little soul!

Children are a little harder than adults to caricature. They have yet to develop so do not have strong facial features or lines, broken noses, beetling eyebrows and such like. And very few are bald!

Go to school
Now then, if you actually visit a school do not lurk about near it. A large gentleman in a blue suit could feel your collar then take you away for questioning. Would a magistrate believe your innocent plea of just wanting to caricature children? Don't risk it. Ask a head teacher for permission or find a friend who lives opposite to a school as I do! To draw the children featured in figure 31 I went into my front room then watched the little darlings pour out to freedom. I first jotted down a fast impression of two girls waiting for parents to steam up in new cars to carry them a few hundred yards to home and comfort. Will modern children forget how to walk? To help you I have drawn two junior sticks. See figure 32.

Have you noticed how some children wander about with coats not quite on, laces undone, school bags trailing and a general

Fig. 31. Two small victims.   **Fig. 32.** Junior sticks

appearance of self-induced neglect? All good stuff to us caricaturists. What do you pick on to exaggerate in a child? Try face shape, clothes, build and hair styles (such as there are).

Fig. 33. Two good subjects.

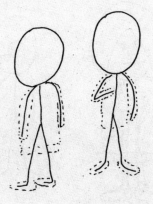

Fig. 34. First impressions.

To give you a further taste of caricaturing children turn your attention to figure 33 with help for you in figure 34. Figures 35 and 36 will provide a little more practice for you. Notice details like hair, eyes, clothes, expressions and face shapes.

Fig. 35.   Draw your version of these children.

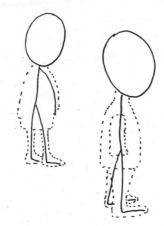

Fig. 36.   More help for you.

You will see that I have not put eyebrows in. The current vogue for hair on some little boys is illustrated in figure 37. Children tend to want their hair done the way their parents' locks are. Unless the adults are bald of course. Draw your version of these children after a look at figure 38.

Fig. 37. Notice details.

Fig. 38. Build from here.

Be fast

It's great fun to dash off quick impressions of children. When they pour out of school they tend to be hyperactive so a fast, careful look followed by swift pencil work could give you some excellent results. My efforts are shown in figure 39.

Fig. 39. First impressions can work.

Notice how I have used shading and a sort of controlled scribble to depict patterns. Draw your version of these children. Start by working out the stick figures.

Assignments
1. From life draw a small child as a caricature.
2. Use your eyes before sketching two older children.
3. Draw a portrait, in caricature, of a child you know.

9

FAMOUS FACES

It is now time to let you loose on the famous. There are, of course, hundreds of world famous people. I have selected just a few who are easy to recognise and caricature.

Entertainers
Sir Elton John, colourful entertainer and personality is known across the world. Look at figure 40, then at the help lines in figure 41, before you draw your version of him. Notice that Sir

Fig. 40. Draw Sir Elton John.

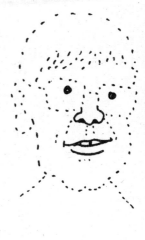

Fig. 41. Help lines for Sir.

Elton has a lop-sided mouth and large glasses which make his eyes seem big.

You may have seen Clive Anderson interviewing various celebrities on his TV show. Figure 42 will show you how to

Fig. 42.   The interrogator.

draw Clive. I think his lawyer's brain gives him a sharp wit. He tends to interrogate his guests for fun. See how I have made his face rather bean-shaped. His wide smile has been exaggerated along with the distinctive eyebrows. You ought to find this face easy to caricature.

Jeremy Clarkson is another popular television personality. For some years he presented the latest, greatest and fastest cars around. He has now moved on to include planes, trains, power boats and all. Doesn't he have a lovely job?

Jeremy's full head of dark, curly hair is a strong feature as

Fig. 43.   Speed merchant

are his eyebrows. Notice in figure 43 how I have treated the hair. This was drawn in with dozens of little squiggly strokes with a pen. Study the big three features in figure 44 before drawing your masterpiece of this happy guy.

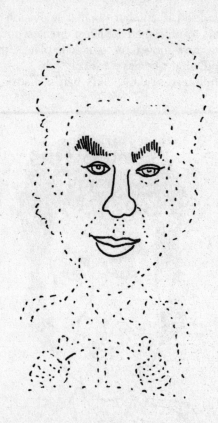

Fig. 44.   Draw the big three accurately.

Another television personality to become famous is the talented comic actor Gregor Fisher who first came to our notice by performing in a number of commercial advertisements for cigars. Then he went on to create a Glaswegian

Fig. 45. Rab C Nesbit.

Fig. 46. Help lines for Rab.

drop-out and loser called Rab C Nesbit. His props for this part include a string vest, ragged coat, grimy headband and wild hairstyle. Look at figure 45. He's a super person to caricature. Start your version by examining figure 46.

007

Any actor who plays the part of James Bond, 007, is assured of world wide coverage and fame. The current Bond has elevated Pierce Brosnan to this high status. His strong, handsome face appealed to the caricaturist within me. Figure 47 will reveal my impression of this fine actor. I exaggerated the length of his face and nose then decided to shade in half the face to give it a bit of drama. I used diagonal lines to shade. After a quick look at figure 48 try your hand at this.

Fig. 47.   007.

Fig. 48. Get the essentials right.

In the news
Some folk are frequently in the news. Dozens in fact, but I
have selected William Hague, Tory leader, because he's
almost always grinning like a schoolboy. This wide smile is
fine to caricature. See figure 49. I like the small teeth just
showing. You might settle on some other feature when you
draw William.

Prime Minister's wife, Cherie Blair, is wonderful to caricature. Why? Look at the unusual shape of the lovely lips shown
in figure 50. The mouth and lips loosely form a figure of eight
on its side. Cherie also has a very distinctive chin line. These
two features are enough to caricature. Almost everyone can
recognise her from these. See how they show up in the lower
help line sketch. Try this. If you get the chin and mouth right
you are there.

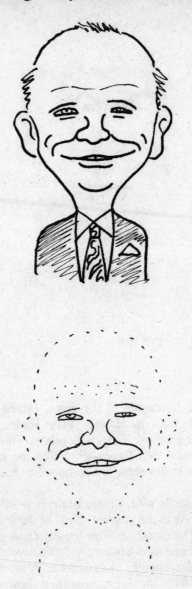

Fig. 49.   A smiling William Hague.

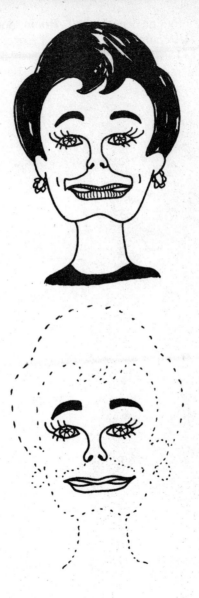

Fig. 50. Above: Lovely Cherie.
Below: Get the mouth right first.

Like many prominent politicians, Robin Cook has a good face to draw. He reminded me of a small terrier type of dog so this is the way I caricatured him. Poor chap! Have a look at figure 51 then re-draw him with a dog's body. Isn't this a giggle?

Fig. 51. Doggy Cook.

Assignments
1. Caricature a famous TV star.
2. Turn your talent to a famous film star.
3. Caricature a person in the news.

10

LATE GREATS

History is littered with late great characters but for this section I have chosen a few of the magic folk who made millions of people laugh and continue to do so years after they died.

Enduring fame
Way back in the roaring twenties three American brothers got together to form a music or vaudeville act. At first it was a tough life for them but then they began to perform in early films. The Marx brothers quickly became world famous. Quite recently I watched one of their old films on television and recalled seeing it as a small child. That's what I call enduring fame.

Groucho Marx outlasted the other brothers to spread his wit through radio, TV and newspapers.

He was a living caricature when attired in his stage gear. He wore a black frock coat, pin-stripe trousers and invented a way of walking with body bent forward from the waist. In one hand, or in his mouth, there was a huge cigar. So here is an easy subject for you to caricature. See figure 52 before grabbing your pencil.

A lovely double act
Shortly after first glimpsing the Marx brothers in movies, I and hundreds of other local kids watched Laurel and Hardy's antics. The children's show was on a Saturday morning. It was

Fig. 52. Groucho – a natural caricature.

commonly known as the Saturday crush.

Stan Laurel was born in Ulverston, Lancashire in 1895. The house in which he was born is open to the public. When I visited it and saw the gloomy, poverty-stricken environment it is in I could picture young Stanley trying to earn a penny or two by trying to be funny in local clubs and pubs.

His partner, Oliver Hardy, was teamed up with Stanley during early silent film days in Hollywood. Their brand of humour included much destruction, chaos and woe through which their child-like innocent reactions shone, then eventually triumphed. Their old films are still shown all over the world. Unlike a good many performers they were sweet natured and admired each other's work.

Oliver was the one who appeared to be neat and tidy. He was forever trying to smarten his pal Stan up. I have drawn them for figure 53. See the lower sketch for help lines.

The first great comic
Charlie Chaplin struggled through appalling poverty in his early years to become astonishingly famous and wealthy as a comical hero of silent films. Before talkies came in, he had become a millionaire. It was his original comedy plus the advent of movies which catapulted him to world fame in a comparatively short time.

He went on to make sound films some of which he wrote, produced, directed and starred in. What a little bundle of extraordinary talent he was. His standard props were a cane, bowler hat, baggy trousers and black jacket. He was another living caricature. When you draw him you can depict him simply by sketching his eyebrows, nose, moustache, cane and bowler hat. Figures 54 and 55 should put you on the right track.

A legendary lady
Mae West was an artist of the Chaplin era. She performed into old age and was an icon of Hollywood. Where would we be without her immortal lines: "Come up and see me sometime"

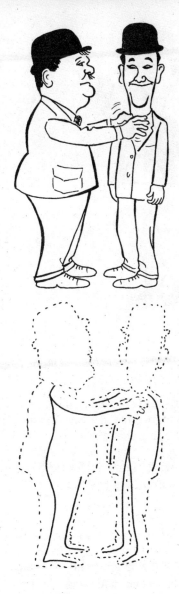

Fig. 53. Above: The immortal Laurel and Hardy.
Below: Help lines for Stan and Oliver.

Fig. 54. Talented Charlie.   **Fig. 55.**   Basic lines for Charlie.

or ''Peel me a grape?'' Her name found its way into the
English language after the Air Sea Rescue Service, in World
War II, named a life jacket a Mae West. Mae often wore huge
wigs for her stage act. I have used this prop in the caricature in
figure 56. The stick figure in figure 57 should help you to
sketch your version of this past star.

Home-grown late greats
Not many comedians have a sort of built-in ability to make
people spontaneously laugh. Big Tommy Cooper, however,
was one man with this magic. Tall, with huge flat feet, he had
only to walk on stage and stare in bewilderment at his
audience to have them falling about. I once spotted him
driving round a city centre. He looked absolutely lost and

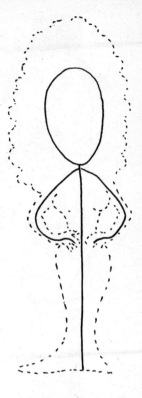

Fig. 56. Dear old Mae West.

Fig. 57. Mae as a stick figure.

puzzled. Made me laugh straight off!

His act mostly consisted of performing conjuring tricks which went wrong while he told rather corny jokes. It seemed to be his appearance, the way that he moved, chuckled and his general air of vulnerability which gained the love of his millions of fans.

Study figure 58. Tommy always wore a fez for his act. I exaggerated his look of horror, feet and face shape for this caricature. Figure 59 is your help line sketch. See what you can do. Then take a tea break.

Fig. 58. Just like that!.   **Fig. 59.** Help lines for Tommy.

Tony Hancock was another home-grown late great comic. Few performers were good enough to stop the nation's normal life so that over twenty million people could listen to a radio show, but Tony did just that with *Hancock's Half-hour*. He then followed radio success with television fame. He had two brilliant writers in Galton and Simpson plus a superb cast of fellow artistes. Insecurity and alcohol, however, caused him to

Fig. 60. Troubled Tony.

abandon his supporting actors Sid James, Kenneth Williams and others. His brilliant script-writers were also given the push. What a great shame.

Figure 60 is my caricature of Tony. For this I exaggerated his mouth, nose and heavily-lidded eyes. Figure 61 should help you to caricature this great comic.

Fig. 61. Help lines for Hancock.

The King

My caricature of Elvis Presley is featured in figure 62. The late lamented Elvis Presley was, of course, the king of rock

Fig. 62.   Elvis the Pelvis.

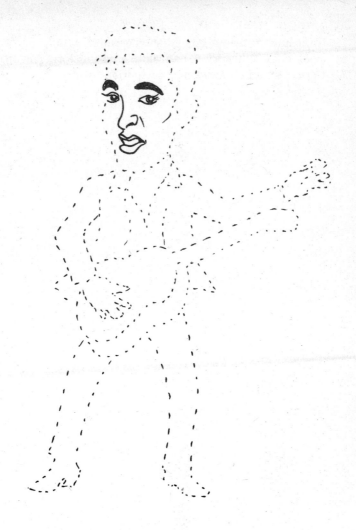

Fig. 63. Help for the King.

and roll. His powerful voice is still heard on the radio almost every day. A really late great. Figure 63 should help you to caricature this legendary star.

Assignments
1. Caricature a famous late great entertainer.
2. Look back in history to caricature a past historic person.
3. Caricature a past sportsman or sportswoman.

11

TURN ON THE TELLY

You need look no further than your TV set to see scores of famous people. With a little practice you can draw quick caricatures of some celebrities. Repeated appearances on television almost always lead to widespread fame for stars and the occasional unknown. Such is the power of the little box.

How to draw from television
Drawing whilst watching TV is a quick way of learning how to observe accurately, and draw the famous. You might like to try my simple method. I have a pile of scrap A5 size paper handy and a 2B drawing pencil. The back of a sketch pad is used to place the scrap paper on. As my victims appear on the screen I dash off fast impressions from as many different angles as possible. As each rough is completed it is dropped on the floor near my chair. When the programme has finished I then sort through the roughs. The best are re-drawn again before selecting a final one to transfer and ink in. You will be surprised how effective this system is after just a little practice. Sometimes one of your roughs will be good enough to use as it is. There are several examples of first roughs in this and other chapters.

Television presenters
Millionaire television and radio presenter Chris Evans is featured in figure 64. This caricature was drawn from

Fig. 64. Presenter Chris Evans.

Fig. 65. The big three for Chris.

television. It was my first rough sketch, but captured what I wanted, so was used this way. The teeth, mouth, glasses and eyebrows were first sketched in. The hair was done with a loose scribble-like effect. Figure 65 shows the Big Three. In quick time draw your version of Mr Evans.

Another well-known presenter – and all-round entertainer – is Rolf Harris. His appearances on *Animal Hospital* have increased his fame and fans. Some years ago I happened to see him demonstrate big brush painting. I drew a quick caricature of him. For the one in figure 66 I just jotted down the

Fig. 66.   Good old Rolf Harris.

important lines whilst watching him on a television screen. Figure 67 will help you to produce a good likeness.

Figure 68 is another caricature drawn from a TV programme. This is a good example of fast, loose sketching which comes off. It could be in the mode of "a poor imitation" which is one description of a caricature. What do you think? See figure 69 for the basic construction lines. Sir David Attenborough, of course, is known all over the world. If you draw his mouth, nose and eyes more or less correctly then your caricature should be fine. Here again we see the addition

Fig. 67. Rolf's basic construction.

Fig. 68. Sir David and friends.

Fig. 69. Help lines for Sir David.

of other characters that can enhance and finish off your comic creation. Ken Dodd is a very funny TV and stage comic. You should find him easy to draw. Note the tickling stick and wild hair. He now uses his battle with the Inland Revenue in his act.

Fig. 70. Draw Doddy.

Fig. 71. Good old Brucie!

Bruce Forsyth has been on our TV screens for decades. He has a face which is known the world over and is fairly easy to caricature. For figure 71 I exaggerated his chin, teeth, nose and eyes. Look at figure 72 before making your caricature of this star.

Peter Snow is the TV presenter who shows the nation the Swingometer on Election night. He also presents other pro-

Fig. 72. Note the distinctive nose!

grammes and is a polished performer. My caricature of him is shown in figure 73 with the help lines in figure 74. I'm sure you will be able to jot down your version of this popular man.

Most mornings whilst at breakfast I listen to popular radio DJ Terry Wogan's bright and funny show. I became one of his millions of fans during his first radio programmes on Radio 2 many years ago. Listeners enjoy his quick wit, other listeners' humorous letters and the general cheerfulness of this show.

Fig. 73. Swingometer operator.

Fig. 74. Notice the eyes and glasses.

Years ago I too sent in witty letters which were broadcast. It's great fun.

Terry, of course, is also a successful TV presenter. It must be nice to have a world fame in both mediums. My caricature of Tel, as he is called by fans, is featured in figure 75. I exaggerated his nose, chin and face shape. Figure 76 should help you to draw your caricature of this pleasant man.

When I taught some years ago I had a very talented cartoonist in my class and used a few of his cartoons in one of my earlier books. We became friends and stayed in touch so it was natural for me to ask John Ball if he could draw caricatures. He said he didn't know but he liked a challenge. I have

Fig. 75. Wogan in the bowels of Broadcasting House.

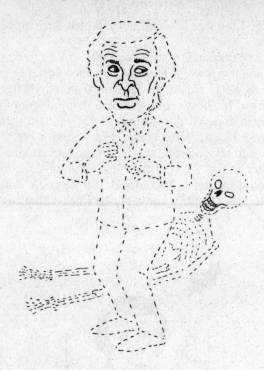

Fig. 76. Help with Terry Wogan.

great pleasure in using his drawings within these pages. How many other folks are out there with hidden talents?

TV host Michael Parkinson has recently returned to present a series of chat shows which draw huge audiences. John Ball has captured Parky interviewing. See figure 77. The stick figure is in figure 78.

A bit of spice
The now world famous Spice Girls are quite good to caricature. The girls have become millionaires through their singing act. I tried to draw my caricature of them quickly and did not bother too much about their figures or clothes. The hard part

Fig. 77. Parky interviewing.

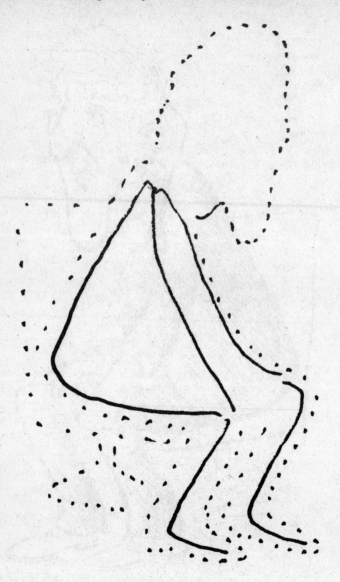

Fig. 78. Help lines for the sitting position.

Fig. 79. A bit of spice is nice.

Fig. 80. Lay out your stick figures.

was fitting them all in a small space. Study figures 79 and 80 before you depict them.

Class

Take a look at figure 81 to see John's caricature of class opera singer Luciano Pavarotti who first came to our notice through televised concerts.

Fig. 81.   Lucky Luciano.

Notice how John has used a bit more humour by sketching in an exploding button. Little things count in this game. John produces his finished drawing by first lightly sketching several pencil roughs on thin layout paper before transferring the final result onto cartridge paper. He uses a dip pen which he combines with a fine-line drawing pen of the sort I use. Look at my help lines in figure 82 before you draw your version of this famous singer.

Fig. 82. The basic lines.

Television always needs good writers. One outstanding TV writer is John Mortimer who brought the joys of *Rumpole of the Bailey* to our screens. My friend John is responsible for the excellent caricature of Mr Mortimer in figure 83. Notice the props John has used to fill in the background. If you would like a challenge try to draw your version of this writer by first planning the construction lines.

Fig. 83. TV writer at work!

Television brought actor, comic, writer, producer and director John Cleese world fame. You may remember his outstanding performances as Basil Fawlty in *Fawlty Towers* which proved to be his springboard to huge success in films. To caricature big John, I exaggerated his chin, eyebrows and face length. One of the supporting actors in the series was Andrew Sachs who played the hapless waiter Manuel. My caricature of

Fig. 84.   Basil (John Cleese) with Manuel (Andrew Sachs).

Manuel is included in figure 84. Glance at the stick figures
(85) before you set to work.

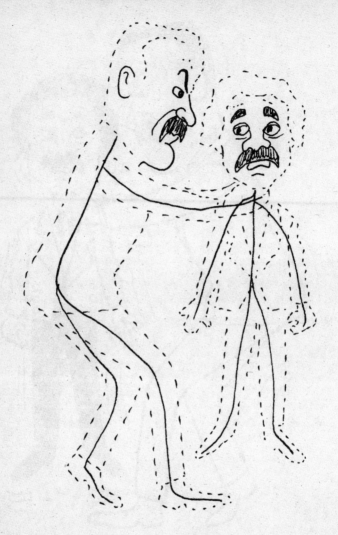

Fig. 85.   The basic lines.

New stars

A fairly recent television performer to shoot up to stardom is Lily Savage as played by Paul O'Grady. He plays the part

Fig. 86.   The outrageous Lily Savage.

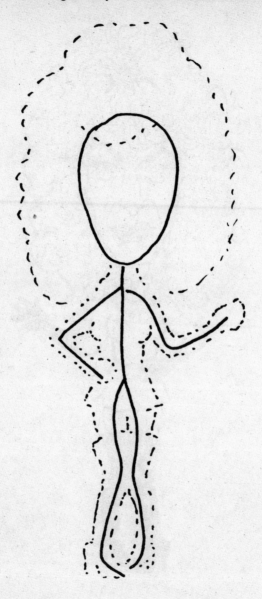

Fig. 87.   Construct Lily.

of an outrageous single mother from Liverpool. His wit is sharp and original. My caricature of him in figure 86 was compiled from photographs and by watching the Lily Savage programmes. Figure 87 should help you with this one.

Fig. 88. Bill Owen (Compo) at the wrong end of Nora Batty's broom.

One of the most popular sit-coms is *Last of the Summer Wine*. The TV series has run for many years. One of the enduring characters of this comedy is Bill Owen who plays the part of Compo. This is another caricature by John. It is shown in figure 88. Notice the use of action lines. Figure 89 will help you to draw your version of this famous star.

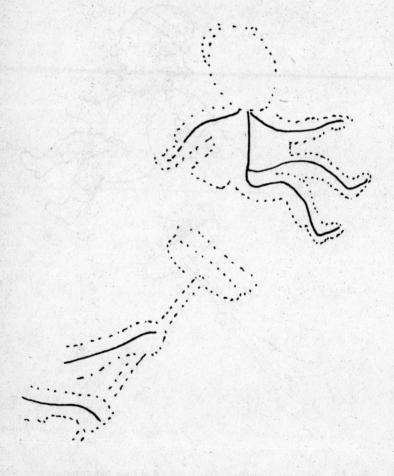

Fig. 89. Basic lines.

Fig. 90. Wisecracking Paul and Ian.

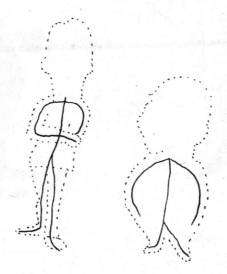

Fig. 91. Sticks to help you.

John has featured two popular TV personalities for his caricature used in figure 90. Paul Merton and Ian Hislop regularly appear in *Have I Got News for You*. Paul also stars in his own comedy series. Notice how effectively John has portrayed the short figure of Ian. Figure 91 gives a bit of help with this one.

Fig. 92. Two famous TV detectives.

Wide fame came to Birmingham comic, Jasper Carrott after he teamed with actor Robert Powell to star in the TV series,

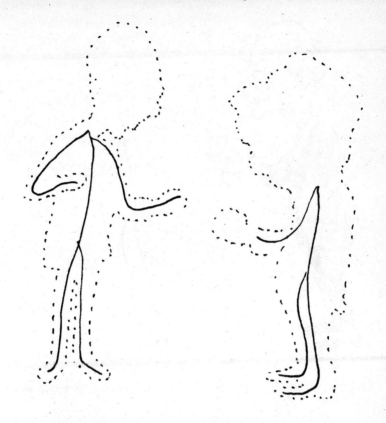

Fig. 93. Jasper and Robert as sticks.

The Detectives. See figure 92. Then study figure 93 before drawing your version of these stars.

Sir John Gielgud, while not strictly a TV actor, became world famous for film and stage roles. A superb all-rounder depicted by John for figure 94. See how shading has been used. See figure 95 for basic lines.

Assignments

1. Watch a TV presenter then quickly caricature the victim.

Fig. 94. Sir John.   **Fig. 95.** An easy figure to draw.

2. Choose a female TV star to caricature.
3. Study a male TV performer before caricaturing him.

12

PLEASE BE A SPORT

You may not have any interest in sport. If this is so try to force yourself to carry out the exercises in this chapter. It will improve your artistic ability. A good caricaturist should be able to tackle any subject.

If you have a favourite sport you will not need my encouragement to caricature your sporting heroes. I'm no different so my choice of victims reflects my interests. For sporting figures I use the type of caricature which is seen in pubs and clubs and once adorned cigarette cards. This is my natural style of drawing.

Fore!

Colin Montgomery has been number one golfer, in Europe, five times. I have had the pleasure of seeing him in action during a few major tournaments. I was too absorbed in the super golf to draw but remember Colin's grim determination to win. I have tried to capture this mood in my sketch for figure 96. I exaggerate his sturdy build, mop of curly hair and nose.

Monty, as he is popularly known, is a superb player. Watching him play was an education. He is able to hit a golf ball a huge distance to land a few feet from the hole. I can't understand why so many of my golf shots hit trees, end up in deep sand or knee-length grass. It's a tough game!

Figure 97 will show you the help lines for this caricature.

Fig. 96. Monty in action.

Notice how to capture action by first getting the stick figure right.

When you draw sportsmen or women you learn about the equipment used, mode of action, clothes and so on.

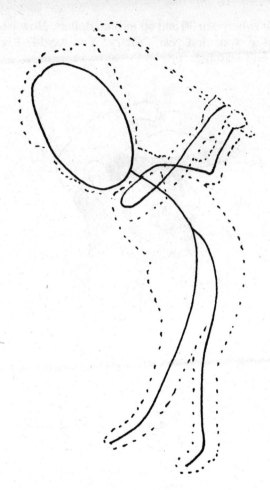

Fig. 97. Help lines for this big man.

A sensational golfer

When young Tiger Woods became a professional golfer in 1997 he broke nine world records and earned more money than any other golfer has in such a short time. The amount has been put at between 30 and 60 million dollars. How would you like that as your first year's salary? You would? Right, rush out for golf lessons!

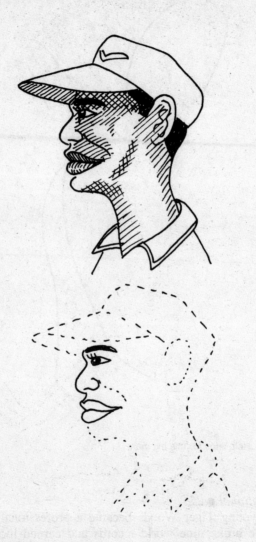

Fig. 98.   Sensational Tiger Woods.

Fig. 99. World star Greg Norman.

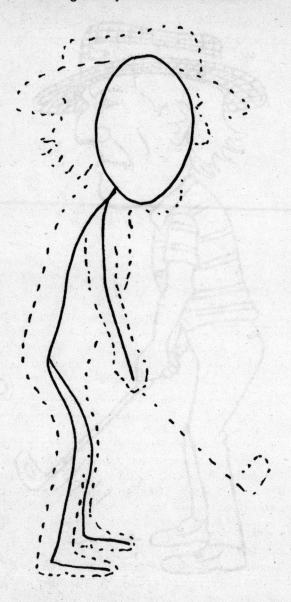

Fig. 100.   This stick figure will help you.

Tiger's talent and exciting play has changed the face of golf worldwide. His presence in a tournament increases fans by over one third. How about that for fame? Mind you, the pressures this youngster is under are more than those of any other sports star. Draw your version of Tiger after studying figure 98.

A world champion
Australian Greg Norman is another golf great I have seen at work. He was World Number One for several years but may be eclipsed by young Tiger Woods. His sport has made him a multi-millionaire, rich enough to buy a jet for his personal use.

Figures 99 and 100 will help you with your caricature of this wonder man.

Everyone for tennis
A British hero to emerge from the tennis season of 1997 and become Sports Personality of the Year – and British Number One – is Greg Rusedski. He's featured in figure 101. His strong eyebrows, distinctive nose and hair style helped to make him easy to caricature. Greg can hit a tennis ball at 140 miles per hour. That's powerful enough to take my head off! Figure 102 should help you to draw the figure correctly.

Young Tim Henman is another Briton to shine through. He won a couple of tournaments in dazzling style to reach the top dogs in international tennis. Figure 103 is of Tim in action. A stick figure, as in figure 104, will help you to make a little masterpiece of this young star.

The top man
Pete Sampras is the American Number One and World Number One at the time of writing. He is another power hitter who can make tennis look easy. His wide smile, strong eyebrows and curly hair should help you to make a quick

Fig. 101. Superstar Greg Rusedski.

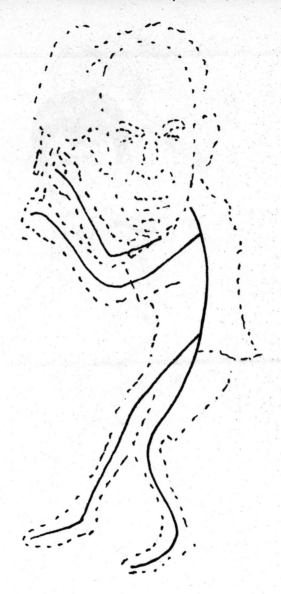

Fig. 102. Get the action right.

Fig. 103.   Tim in action.

caricature of him. See figure 105 and figure 106 for the basic construction.

Fig. 104.   Stick figures help with action figures.

We each have a hero
Steve Davis is my favourite snooker player. Watching him win snooker tournaments prompted me to try to learn how to play his game. I soon discovered that it wasn't my game.

Fig. 105. Mighty Pete.

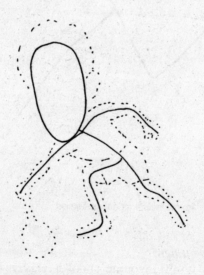

Fig. 106. Basic structure for the champ!

Fig. 107. Champion Steve.

Instead of spending a misspent old age in smoke-filled snooker halls I returned to the sport of golf. It was for the best.

Figure 107 depicts my caricature of past world champion Steve who is still pulling in the crowds. He seems a very nice guy. Study the guide lines in figure 108 before you draw him.

Fig. 108. Help with Davis.

Fig. 109. Botham hurtles down the pitch . . .

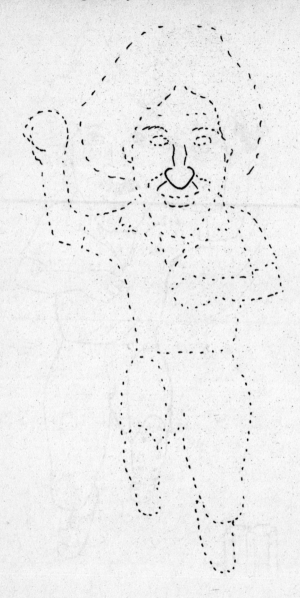

Fig. 110. Help lines for Ian.

Fig. 111. Know what I mean, Harry?

Fig. 112.   A challenge for you!

All-round cricket legend Ian Botham is my sporting hero. Back in the eighties I remember being glued to my TV screen to watch him, against all odds, win a test match against the Australians. Figure 109 shows Ian hurtling up to bowl. He was also a first-class batsman and fielder. Notice the flowing locks which he then wore. Basic construction lines are in figure 110.

Boxing is not one of my favourite sports but I think that big

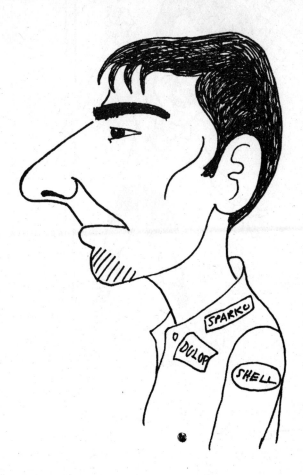

Fig. 113. Over the Hill?

Fig. 114. England's goalkeeper.

Frank Bruno was a worthy champion who also turned out to shine in the entertainment industry. Know what I mean? A BBC sports commentator sort of linked up with Frank so I

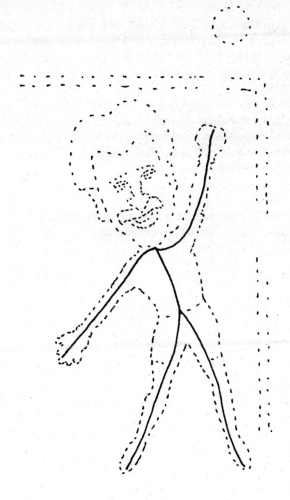

Fig. 115. David's basic construction.

have drawn little Harry Carpenter with him for figure 111. See
how I have used tiny circles to depict Bruno's hair. Figure 112
should help you to draw a good caricature of this famous pair.

Easy ones for you

Fast man Damon Hill has a super face to caricature. See figure 113. Notice the Big Three. You should be able to draw, with one eye closed, your version of this great driver who is a past world champion. You won't need any help lines for this one. Go for it.

David Seaman, goalkeeper for England is my choice to represent footballers in this book. He has a very individual hair style, moustache and happy grin which make caricaturing him relatively easy. Take a look at figures 114 and 115 before putting your skill to use.

Assignments

1. Draw a caricature of a famous sportsman.
2. Caricature a famous sportswoman.

13

MAKE A BIT OF DOSH

Most beginner caricaturists, due to a lack of confidence, never consider ways of making money with their newly acquired skill. It can be good fun, however, caricaturing your chums in exchange for a small fee or even drinkies. My advice is to stay cool and use your humour in a light-hearted way to obtain payment of some sort.

How to make money with caricatures
If you want to try to make a little loot with your skill think of making a modest start. Forget about becoming an instant overnight national caricaturist straight off. This will take loads of practice, talent and a bit of luck.

How to start
First get together a good selection of your finished work. Be business-like. Present your gems attractively by using a proper portfolio rather than wrapping in old newspapers. So what's next? Find a customer in your locality. This could be a well-known councillor, or council, a sports personality, maybe local big-shot businessman, publican, or local major or minor celebrity. Try clubs, pubs and any outfit where there are people.

Most people with a sense of humour and normal intelligence are flattered when asked if they could be caricatured. You might try this path to begin with, but don't make the big

Fig. 116.   Big-shot businessman ballooning.

mistake of drawing for nothing. You are a professional. Charge a small fee or even a payment in kind. I was once paid in Book Tokens for a caricature of a retiring boss.

Your local newspaper may consider your stuff. If it's really good, commissions to caricature local folk could be offered by the editor.

Fig. 117. A final look at Robin Cook.

Last hints

Keep on drawing. Do not give up if at first you get a caricature wrong. All the drawing you have now done during this course will have increased your powers of observation and accuracy of drawing.

My chum John and I lost count of the number of failed rough sketches we made before managing to obtain a reasonable caricature of some victims. Remember that John had never tried caricaturing until I asked him to have a go. I have used two of his gems to finish this book with. See figures 116 and 117.

Thank you for being my student. Good luck to you.